HOW TO READ A COMIC BOOK

Comic books are made up of pictures in boxes, called panels. Look at each of these panels from left to right, and top to bottom.

Read the speech bubbles, caption boxes and any sound effects from left to right, too. Together with the images, these will tell you the story.

CHAPTER FOUR:
MR CHUNK

GARDEN & AQUATICS
CENTRE
ENTRANCE

@EXIT

It was Saturday again, and I was back at the garden centre with Mum. Only this time, Knots was with me.

Oh, look, a sale on plastic flowers.

Norman, you stay here.

That was my chance to investigate.

Do you know what the gnome hunters look like?

One was tall and thin, the other was short and fat, and they both smelled really bad.

I knew the plastic flowers wouldn't keep mum busy for long.

MUMBLE MUMBLE

We needed to find them fast.

13

CHAPTER SIX:
NOW WE GNOME

As soon as we were home, Knots and I looked over the picture for any clues.

Knots spotted it. A web address!

I brought up the website on the computer.

Look, an address. That is just around the corner from here. Let's go Monday morning.

Gulp, OK.

CHAPTER EIGHT: THE BIG PLAN

As I walked the rest of the way to school, Knots filled me in on his plan.

For the first part of the plan, we were going to need to send an email.

To: contact@flakeandchunk.com

Subject: Adverts

Dear Mr Flake and Mr Chunk. My name is Mr Megabucks and I make free television adverts for companies that I like. If you would like a free advert, please meet me at your gnome factory at 10 o'clock tomorrow evening. P.S. Dress like gnomes.

Yours sincerely, Mr Megabucks.

I should have been frightened, but I was excited. This was anything but normal.

That evening I told Mum...

... I'm going out to play on my bike.

The next part of the plan was to find more gnomes...

... lots more gnomes!

I would smash the gnomes free from their shells and Knots would fill them in on the plan and tell them to meet us at my house.

We did this for hours. I didn't like breaking other people's property, but gnomes weren't property — they were people.

But soon it was time to head home.

When I got home, I rushed up to my room.

CHAPTER NINE:
THE DAY OF THE GNOMES

The next night, I snuck out after bedtime and headed to the gnome factory.

Actually stood there in front of the gnome factory, I was a bit scared.

I have to do this for Knots. He is my best friend.

Right, lads. You all know what you need to do!

Dad's wide brimmed hat.

Paintbrush bristles.

Shades.

Dad's old overcoat.

KNOCK
KNOCK

I thought I made quite a good Mr Megabucks in my makeshift disguise.

Now Chunk noticed the gnomes on the shelves.

You should have left the gnomes alone.

This is all your fault!!!

I didn't know this was going to happen!

Quick! Run!

He's there, get him!

@2022 BookLife Publishing Ltd.
King's Lynn, Norfolk PE30 4LS

ISBN 978-1-80155-054-3

All rights reserved. Printed in Poland.
A catalogue record for this book is
available from the British Library.

Day of the Gnomes
Written by Robin Twiddy
Illustrated by Kel Winser

ABOUT BOOKLIFE GRAPHIC READERS

BookLife Graphic Readers are designed to encourage reluctant readers to take the next step in their reading adventure. These books are a perfect accompaniment to the BookLife Readers phonics scheme and are designed to be read by children who have a good grasp on reading but are reluctant to pick up a full-prose book. Graphic Readers combine graphic and prose storytelling in a way that aids comprehension and presents a more accessible reading experience for reluctant readers and lovers of comic books.

ABOUT THE AUTHOR

Robin is a lifelong comic book fan whose love for the medium led to it being the topic of his undergraduate dissertation. He is the author of many great BookLife titles, including several entries into the BookLife phonic reader scheme. Robin loves action, adventure and humour and brings these elements together into exciting narratives you won't forget.

ABOUT THE ILLUSTRATOR

Kel has been drawing cartoons, superheroes and comics for as long as he can remember. He divides his time between teaching the next generation of cartoonists, making illustrations and comics for himself and publishers, spending time with his family, and growing an enormous beard! Kel lives in Norwich, UK with his wife and son.